Magical Energy in the Gnostic Mass

Magical Energy in the Gnostic Mass
Frater IAO131

DEADMAN PUBLISHING

Houghton, Michigan
2017

ISBN 978-0-9827014-4-7

Dead Man Publishing, LLC
400 Agate Street
Houghton, MI 49931

Cover design by Frater Yeheshuah

An Introduction

Do what thou wilt shall be the whole of the Law!

Magickal energy is not an easy subject to tackle in any scholarly manner. And yet, the magician recognizes that energy in her more successful moments in ritual and meditation. The difficulty in speaking of magickal energy is not so much in uncovering moments of its appearance, but in properly characterizing the phenomenon. As a poet, a philosopher and a magician, I realize a sort of continuity in the energies worked up and released by the hard work of picking apart and reconstructing a poem, in the energies that fill the body with lightness after the dawning of a philosophical idea that turns a jumble of propositions into the derivation of a necessary truth, in the energies of invoking Horus so thoroughly as to be convinced that the god of the morning sun is alive in me. If these energies are continuous with one another, it makes little sense to appeal to an amorphous and unclear concept of magickal energy when psychology and physiology provide us with all we need to make sense of the various phenomena in question.

Intellectual skepticism is generally taken to be one of the hallmarks of Thelema. However, Thelema does not require a constant skeptical vigilance, as practices such as those outlined in *Liber Astarte* virtually demand the offering of oneself in faith to the worship of a particular deity. Such offerings may originally be made against the background of skepticism and experimentation, but it is my experience that we can easily become lost in our adopted religious world. The skeptical origins of one's religious practice slips into the past and the magician finds herself an unquestioning devotee of Kali or Odin or Adonai. Without a record of where we began, we risk being overwhelmed by the hypnotic power of religion. (This risk of losing oneself is why, I believe, Crowley warns: "It may occur that owing to the tremendous power of the Samadhi, overcoming all other memories as it should and does do, that the mind of the devotee may be obsessed, so that he declare his particular Deity to be sole God and Lord." (*Astarte*, 43) Crowley also writes that we ought to construct our place of worship to remind us that the Supreme transcends all religions and all categories: "with regard to the Deity also, there should be some one affirmation of his identity both with all other similar gods of other nations, and with the Supreme of whom all are but partial reflections." (*Astarte*, 2))

Bhakti practices, such as that outlined in *Liber Astarte*, are overwhelming in their capacity to enflame the soul in prayer. With that said, I would be hard pressed to articulate a case for viewing those energies as anything more than the peculiarities of the human brain and body. It is, of course, rather useless to introspect with regard to such matters. The privilege of having a body and a brain gives me no privileged access to their operations. That is the domain of psychologists and cognitive scientists. At best, I can try to describe the kind of experiences I have when engaged in magickal and mystical work. And even there, I am afraid, I am likely to get the matter wrong. But where else can we begin?

The selection presented here from *Hriliu: Symbolic Explorations of the Gnostic Mass* by Frater IAO131 works to give that first, tentative description of magickal energy. IAO131 delves into two main questions: how do we describe the concept of magickal energy and how does magickal energy manifest itself in our experience? The first half of "Magickal Energy" walks through the various concepts magicians (as well as the mystics of the world's various religious traditions) use to talk about magickal power. After that conceptual section, we turn to the metaphysics of magickal force.

IAO131's approach as I have described it is theoretical in nature, but I do not believe he is primarily a theoretician. IAO131's work (and I am basing this conclusion on more than just the work we see here) seems to stem from a devoted magickal practice. He is a practitioner, a magician. Much like the Fathers of the Patristic era, IAO131 is grappling with magickal experience; the theory is second to the devotion. The theory therefore is not necessarily systematic or fully developed. IAO131 is tackling questions very few have yet tried to take on. This is because

Thelema is just in its infancy. Few people have taken up Thelema, and even fewer have tried to develop Thelema with regard to either theory or practice. New ground is being broken. A new temple is being raised.

Having noted the analogy with the Patristic era, we must take into account IAO131's writing first as a devotee of Thelema, and then, second, as a theologian or philosopher. As Christianity developed, any and all resources were made use of to describe the experience of faith. Neo-Platonic philosophy, Greek poetry, Essene asceticism were all incorporated in an increasingly large and diverse set of Christianities. There was no grand philosophical structure or creed that governed the Christian Church. Whatever aided the Christian devotee to develop and enhance her faith experience was worth adopting. So it is with IAO131. He turns to psychology and comparative religion and phenomenology as he sees fit. He does not sift the sands as carefully as would a PhD thesis on Thelema. But that is not his intent. His writing is an attempt to articulate his wrestling with magick, a magick that is first practiced and then talked about. IAO131 has asked questions without giving definitive answers, granting us permission to approach Thelema critically… and devotedly.

Dead Man Publishing sees "Magickal Energy" as the appropriate beginning to our new chapbook series, which we hope will see experts of all stripes taking on Thelemic philosophy and religion critically. This essay by IAO131 sits somewhere between devotional writing and theoretical work. His work is the bridge between our practice and our understanding.

We will not fail to respond critically to what we love with deep devotion. We have the method of science and the aim of religion.

Fraternally,

Frater Yeheshuah

Love is the law, love under will.

MAGICAL ENERGY IN
THE GNOSTIC MASS

I. WHAT IS MAGICAL ENERGY?

The Gnostic Mass - like virtually all ceremonial rituals - utilizes what is called "magical energy," "magical force," or "magical power." This magical energy is a mysterious force that operates under the control of the Magician, the individual who consciously employs it to effect his or her magical ends. The nature of magical energy is obscure, and it is often described in multiple, sometimes contradictory ways. We may begin to understand what magical force is, at least its theoretical aspects, by understanding how Crowley understood and used the term in various ways.

Prana

Magical force is understood in one way as "prana," the Hindu term for energy. *Prana* has been called "energy," the "life-force," or the "vitalizing principle" of the universe, and it has its particular expression in the microcosm of Man. *Prana* as the life-force is therefore connected with the idea of breath, or the "breath of life," which is a name for the vitalizing principle of Life in various systems. For the Hindus it is *prana,* for the Chinese it is *chi,* for the Japanese it is *ki,* and for the Hebrew it is *ruach*: all these terms essentially equate "breath" and "spirit" or "life-force." In this way, we may liken it to that which is mentioned in the Creed of the Gnostic Mass, "I believe... in one Air the nourisher of all that breathes." Sabazius reinforces this interpretation in his commentary to this line of the Creed, "As the *Ruach*, it is the Holy Spirit, the Mind of the Formative World, and the Son of the Father, which caresses the cheek of our fair Mother, and which descends from the sky to mediate between us and our Father the Sun by communicating the Holy *Prana* into our blood through Inspiration."

This connection between breath and *prana,* or magical force, is the rationale for the practice of *pranayama,* which involves the regularization and control of the breath. *Pranayama* is not technically the control of *prana* directly, but it is the control of *prana* through the control of breath, which is understood as a primary vehicle of *prana. Pranayama* tends to produce a certain kind of sweat which can be seen as a parallel to or identified with that spoken of in THE BOOK OF THE LAW: "...the dew of her light bathing his whole body in a sweet-smelling perfume of sweat."[1] This connection will be further developed in the next main section of this essay.

Aud

There is a particular tripartite division of Light utilized in the Hermetic Order of the Golden Dawn, which uses three different terms to describe different "types" or "aspects" of force: Aub, Aud, and Aur. This Order and its tenets obviously influenced Crowley's thinking greatly.

Aub is a kind of lunar force, associated with the terms "Obi" and "obeah," and Crowley calls it "the astral light... an illusory thing of witchcraft (cf. Obi, Obeah)... [which is] sluggish, vicious"[2] and "the secret Fire of Obeah."[3]

This is contrasted with *Aud,* which is called "Special 'fire' or 'light' of the Sacred Magic of Light, Life, and Love; hence 'Odic Force'"[4] and "Aud is almost = the Kundalini force ('Odic' force)... [which is] "keen, ecstatic."[5] Aud is specifically the form of Light or force that is understood as "magical force" - reinforced by the fact that Aud (dw)) enumerates to 11, the number of Magick; he also equates it with the Kundalini force within Mankind (which we will come back to in a moment).

Aur is generally a term used for Light in general and

---

1   *Liber AL,* I:27.
2   *Liber LVIII.*
3   *Liber Aleph.*
4   *Sepher Sephiroth.*
5   *Liber LVIII: Gematria.*

specifically refers to Divine Light - it is associated with "Ain Soph Aur," the Limitless Light that forms the 3rd Negative Veil of Existence on the Qabalistic tree of Life. In the Golden Dawn system, which Crowley undoubtedly picked up on and utilized, the Practicus $3°=8^{\square}$ ritual explains that Aub, Aud, and Aur are the threefold forms of Fire (understood here as another name for Light or force). The Aub is the "Astral" and "Passive" form of Fire, Aud is the "Volcanic" and "Active" form of Fire, and Aur is the "Solar" and "Equilibrated" form of Fire. We might symbolize these three forces in the microcosm as the passive & undirected force in Man (Aub), the active & directed force in Man (Aud), and the Divine or macrocosmic force that imposes upon Man in ecstasy and illumination (Aur).

Within the context of magical ritual, and the Gnostic Mass in particular, it can be understood that "magical force" is understood as Aud, the active and directed form of force, directed by the intent of the Magician. This is confirmed in LIBER ALEPH where Crowley writes of the symbol of the Lion, "Of this, Lion, o my Son, be it said that this is the Courage of thy Manhood, leaping upon all Things, and seizing them for their Prey... in The Book of Thoth He is the Atu called Strength [or 'Lust' when he final;y created his Thoth Tarot], whose Number is ELEVEN which is Aud, the Light Odic of Magick. And therein is figured the Lion, even THE BEAST, and Our Lady BABALON astride of Him, that with her Thighs She may strangle Him." There is, of course, also the cryptic note at the end of Crowley's discussion of ATU XI: Lust in THE BOOK OF THOTH which reads, "Further study of this card may be made by close examination of LIBER XV [i.e. The Gnostic Mass]." There is thus a direct connection between Aud, 11, ATU XI: Lust, and the Gnostic Mass in particular.

Kundalini

Kundalini is the "serpent power" within each individual which lies dormant, coiled 3 ½ times in the Muladhara chakra at the base of the spine. It represents the magical force of Man which is awakened and brought progressively up the spine to the Ajna chakra in the forehead (the "third eye") wherein it unites with the "Lord of All," and the bliss of *samadhi* or ecstatic union of subject and object occurs.

We have seen already that Crowley equates the active, directed magical force of Aud with Kundalini. Further, the equation of Kundalini with *prana* is frequent in many texts, and their connection is often explained by the fact that Kundalini is the *prana* as manifested in the microcosm of Man. Kundalini is an idea tied up very closely with those of Shiva and Shakti, as well as the cosmological notions that they imply. Very briefly, Shiva is the formless, inert, boundless and infinite Godhead that is Unmanifest, whereas Shakti (which literally means "power") is the force and form, active, boundless and infinite Godhead that is Manifest; they are always understood to be One, Shiva-Shakti, and their separation is only due to ignorance. A Qabalistic analogy would be that the Negative Veils, or Naught, is Shiva, and any deviation from that Naught would be Shakti, including the 1, the initial Positive manifestation; Crowley likens them to the Tao (Shiva) and the Teh (Shakti) in his *Tao Teh Ching;* in Thelemic ontology, Shiva would be 0 and Shakti would be 2 (or That which causes things to appear as 2). Certain sects of Hindus therefore believe that the entire universe is the Manifestation of Shakti, which is another way of saying the world is a manifestation of Power (Nietzsche was about a millenium behind the Hindus with that particular thought).

Shakti is understood to be manifested in Man (meaning the human individual) as Shakti-Kundalini, the serpent-power aforementioned, and it is by her rising up the spine to unite with her Lord Shiva in the Ajna that enlightenment is attained. Therefore, Kundalini is understood as the manifestation of Power ("Shakti") or Life (*prana*) in the individual.

Is Kundalini Male or Female?

It is notable that this serpent-power of magical energy or force is explicitly identified as the "feminine" Shakti, whereas it is common in Western thought to associate power/activity with the masculine and receptivity/passivity to the feminine. A parallel is found, of course, in Babalon and the Scarlet Woman in whom "is all power given"[6] and who is "girt with a sword."[7] The Priestess in the Gnostic Mass is identifiable with Shakti-Kundalini, especially at certain points (although it should be said that both Priestess and Priest very clearly interact and identify with this Serpent force at various times). To name the most obvious examples, the Priestess circumambulates the Temple 3 ½ times before descending to the Tomb, reflecting the Kundalini serpent that is coiled 3 ½ times at the base of the spine. The Priestess is literally girt with a sword, identifying her with the Scarlet Woman in whom "is all power [Shakti] given." More subtly, the Priestess gives the sign of the descending triangle when placed upon the Summit of the Earth (the High Altar), which is the symbol of Ra-Hoor-Khuit but it is also the special symbol of Shakti called the Trikona which appears depicted inside several *chakras* (centers of force infused by Shakti-Kundalini) in the spine. There is also the fact that she is an ecstatic female figure that appears above the Priest, just as Shakti is depicted "riding" Shiva in sexual embrace which is essentially the same in essence as Babalon riding the Beast in "ATU XI: Lust."

The Priest, too, is identified with "magical force" in various ways: he is crowned with a Serpent as a crown which reflects the illumination of the Yogi when the Serpent Kundalini reaches the brow. In LIBER AL, Hadit identifies himself with the Serpent in several places, showing Hadit is manifested as magical force in the symbolic form of the Serpent. The Priest identifies himself with Hadit on the second step toward the Veil. Further, the Priest carries the Lance which is symbolic of the Middle Pillar of the Tree of Life and all *axis mundi* figures (such as "the world-ash wonder tree" symbol of Yggdrasil utilized in the Anthem of the Mass): in certain Hindu texts that discuss Kundalini, the spine of the Yogi with its *chakras* is identified with Mount Meru, a form of the "Holy Mountain" *axis mundi* archetype that can also be seen in the symbols of Mount Zion of the Hebrews, Mount Olympus of the Greeks, and Mount Abiegnus of the Rosicrucians (to name but a

---

6   *Liber AL,* I:15.
7   *Liber AL,* III:11.

few). The Lance is therefore symbolic of manifested magical force, the Kundalini "extended", which is reinforced by the fact that the Priest invokes Nuit "by seed, and root, and stem, and bud, and leaf, and flower, and fruit" which can be considered to be symbolic reflections of the 7 *chakras* depicted as various forms of a Tree, of which the Lance is a symbol. Consider these things in relation to what Crowley remarks in *Magick:*

> *"The Serpent which is coiled about the Crown means many things, or, rather, one thing in many ways. It is the symbol of royalty and of initiation, for the Magician is anointed King and Priest [as the Priest in the Mass]. It also represents Hadit... The serpent is also the Kundalini serpent, the Magical force itself, the manifesting side of the Godhead of the Magician [Shakti], whose unmanifested side is peace and silence [Shiva], of which there is no symbol. In the Hindu system the Great Work is represented by saying that this serpent, which is normally coiled at the base of the spine [Muladhara chakra], rises with her [Shakti's] hood over the head of the Yogi [reflected in the Priest's cap of maintenance], there to unite with the Lord of all [Shiva]."* [8]

The Redemptive Force

We can therefore see an identity between the Serpent, Kundalini, Hadit, and magical force. To these we may add the "Aud" of Magick and the *prana,* at least as it is specifically manifested in the individual. Further symbolism can be understood when Shakti or Kundalini is understood as the Redeemer: it is the force which liberates the Yogi from the cycle of rebirth of *samsara* and the illusion of *maya.* In this way, it is - to use the Western equivalent - the Messiah, or one might say "the messianic force" or "redemptive force." Crowley writes:

> *"In Daath is said to be the Head of the great Serpent Nechesh or Leviathan, called Evil to conceal its Holiness.*

---

8   *Liber ABA*, Part II, chapter 9.

(NChSh [Serpent] = 358 = xy#m [Messiah], the Messiah or Redeemer, and ntywl [Leviathan] = 496 = twklm [Malkuth], the Bride. It is identical with the Kundalini of the Hindu Philosophy, the Kwan-se-on of the Mongolian Peoples, and means the magical Force in Man, which is the sexual Force applied to the Brain, Heart, and other Organs, and redeemeth him." [9]

We therefore see an identity between Kundalini, the magical Force in Man, the Messiah, and the Serpent Nechesh. Crowley also adds in this quotation that this is "the sexual Force." In the Hindu understanding, the sexual force is but one form - although perhaps the most powerful and volatile form - of Shakti or Kundalini, as Shakti is "power" itself and represents all Force, both in the Macrocosm of the Universe and in the Microcosm of Man. Undoubtedly, this is also true in our system, but we recognize the sexual Force as the most potent manifestation of magical Force in general, and it should be clear that the Gnostic Mass utilizes this sexual aspect of Kundalini, or magical force. Even in the Hindu system, Shakti is represented in sexual coition (called *maithuna*) with Shiva, signifying their ecstatic union. The parallel with the Priest and Priestess is likely obvious to most.

Two Additional Points

In closing this brief exploration, there are two notes to make that may seem obvious to some readers but are still worthwhile to point out. Firstly, it is worth repeating that this magical force, or Kundalini or Aud or whatever name we wish to call it, is within both the Priest and Priestess. On the material plane, this means that all individuals, regardless of their biological sex, possess Kundalini or magical force. According to Hindu doctrine, if one did not have this force in some measure, one would be dead since it is the vivifying life-force itself. In our terminology, "Every man and every woman is a star," and also "I believe... in one Air the nourisher of all that breathes." If anything, this Kundalini is in all but expresses itself in different ways, different formulas of force

---

9   *Liber LVIII: Gematria.*

for the different sexes: the we might call these the "formulas" of the *lingam* and *yoni,* which are ritualistically depicted in the Lance and Cup of the Priest and Priestess.[10] Both are necessary for the accomplishment of the magical goal of the Mass. As Crowley writes, "The soul is beyond male and female as it is beyond Life and Death. Even as the Lingam and the Yoni are but diverse developments of One Organ..."[11] This parallels the notion that the "**PHALLUS**," another term used often by Crowley which is equated with Kundalini and magical power, is actually bi-gendered and not solely the property of biological males. The Phallus is properly understood not as the *lingam,* but as the *lingam-yoni.*[12] We can therefore see that "the sole vice-rent of the Sun upon the Earth" is the Generative power of "every man and every woman," reflected ritualistically into the interactions between Priest (*lingam*) and Priestess (*yoni*).

Secondly, it is worth nothing that, although this sexual aspect of magical force is utilized in the Mass, there is no sexual contact - let alone sexual intercourse - in the Mass itself. This implies that the symbolic enactment thereof contains magical force in itself, and it is not simply the physical acts of sexuality that are identifiable with Kundalini, magical force, etc. Even in their symbolic depiction - for example, in the stroking of the Lance or its depression into the Cup - they are not simply "blinds" for physical sex; on the contrary, the acts of physical sex are material

---

10 It is notable that many Priests describe their experience of the Mass as a kind of contraction into a point, and many Priestesses describe their experience as one of expansion, which reflect the magical Images of Hadit and Nuit, respectively, as in "In the sphere I am everywhere the centre, as she, the circumference, is nowhere found... I am the Magician and the Exorcist. I am the axle of the wheel, and the cube in the circle. 'Come unto me' is a foolish word: for it is I that go." (*AL*, II:7)

11 *The Book of Lies,* chapter 35.

12 This identity between the Phallus and Lingam-Yoni is seen through Greek isopsephy where the phrase "O PhALLE" (as in the Star Ruby) in Greek is equal to the value of the words "PhALLOS" (*lingam*) and "KTEIS" (*yoni*) added together. [Ω ΦΑΛΛΕ = 1366; ΦΑΛΛΟΣ = 831; ΚΤΕΙΣ = 535; therefore: 831+535 = 1366.]

manifestations of higher principles, the striving toward the union of subject and object in *samadhi*, the union of Shakti and Shiva in the fully risen Kundalini. Consider what Crowley says about the actual, physical act of sex and its ritualistic use in his essay "Energized Enthusiasm," let alone what that implies for symbolic or ritualistic depictions of sex:

> *"In the sacramental and ceremonial use of the sexual act, the divine consciousness may be attained... Admit [sex's] religious function, and one may at once lay down that the act must not be profaned. It must not be undertaken lightly and foolishly without excuse...*
>
> *I need hardly emphasize the necessity for the strictest self-control and concentration on their part. As it would be blasphemy to enjoy the gross taste of the wine of the sacrament, so must the celebrant suppress even the minutest manifestation of animal pleasure... the sexual excitement must be suppressed and transformed into its religious equivalent...*
>
> *It is, indeed, of the first importance for the celebrant in any phallic rite to be able to complete the act without even once allowing a sexual or sensual thought to invade his mind."*[13]

One might say this all really reduces to, and all naturally follows from the simple and sublime injunction, "Be not animal; refine thy rapture!"[14]

Summary

The essential point, to summarize our various tangents, is that sexuality and the sexual force are form of magical force (or Kundalini) and possibly its most powerful form thereof; magical force is, after all, equated with the life-force and sex is the act by which life perpetuates itself. Nonetheless, the sexual force must be conscious, controlled, and directed for it to be properly considered "magical force." This will be further explored in the next main

---

13 *Liber DCCXI: Energized Enthusiasm.*
14 *Liber AL,* III:70.

---

section of this essay. The Gnostic Mass is a sacred rite wherein this magical force as manifested in sexuality is utilized ritualistically to accomplishment its magical ends.

What is it really, though?

The preceding discussion of magical force or energy was to show that this idea has many names and has appeared in many systems. It is *prana, chi, ki, ruach,* and *kundalini;* it is called variously "magical energy," "magical force," or "magical power"; it is often identified with the sexual force or seen as manifested particularly strongly in sexuality. Nonetheless, what is magical force really?

Crowley discusses this briefly in *Magick in Theory & Practice* where he writes, "Prana or 'force' is often used as a generic term for all kinds of subtle energy...There is some ground for the belief that there is a definite substance (This substance need not be conceived as 'material' in the crude sense of Victorian science...)"[15] It is conceived as a subtle energy that may not be "material" - that is, it does not operate on matter in the way that gravity or electromagnetism do. Around the turn of the 20th century, it was popular for magical force in general to be explained by a sort of "aether", often identified with the now-discarded scientific theory of the luminiferous aether, wherein travels "magical force" or "astral light" or whatever similar terminology. Since the aether is not an empirical construct, this explanation can only remain a kind of quaint metaphor for whatever-it-is that is really going on - it is retained in the Gnostic Mass itself in the line "Let this offering be borne upon the waves of Aethyr..." If magical force or *prana* is an objective force in some way, even if "non-material" in some sense, then it won't be able to be measured with typical measurement tools which, of course, measure material things.

This also relates to the tendency to attribute the *chakras* to various physiological correlates such as nerve plexuses: aside from

---

15 *Magick in Theory & Practice,* chapter 12.

these facts being constantly skewed by authors so that they fit their theories, there is no clean correlation of *chakras* to nerve plexuses in the body, and the Hindus themselves insist that the *chakras* and the Kundalini that may invigorate them are a form of "subtle", i.e. not material, force. They are, in the end, misguided attempts to validate a spiritual experience and practice by trying to show how it supposedly fits into the current materialistic paradigm of science. On this front of seeing *prana* and/or *chakras* as material in some way, we must hold our tongues, at least until there is some way to possibly measure such a force that has essentially eluded scientists to this day.

There is another possible approach, which is that the notion of "energy" springs from a subjective, first-hand experience of some kind. This first-hand experience might be called a "phe-nomenological fact" in the same way that one experiences pain, sadness, or excitement and no knowledge of any physiology is required to justify the fact that pain, sadness, or excitement are *felt* as real. That is to say: people have an experience of feeling something like "energy" or "magical force" moving within their own minds and bodies, and this has been given the name *prana, chi, kundalini,* etc.

"*Tantric Feast*" (circa 179

The very fact that an almost identical phenomenon has been described and has names in various languages attests that this - at least the *experience* of energy in some form - is basically universal across cultures. In a sense, this is what is important to ritual and magick in general as it is the first-hand, direct experience of the individual which counts. If the experience of the Priest, for example, is that certain words, movements, and thoughts lead to an experience of magical energy and its manipulation to experience certain things, such as the "movement" of energy or its culmination in ecstasy, then it does not matter at all whether this magical force is material, non-material, subjective, objective, or anything else. In Crowley's words from LIBER O, "It is immaterial whether these exist or not. By doing certain things certain results will follow; students are most earnestly warned against attributing objective reality or philosophic validity to any of them." Therefore, we may most beneficially take a pragmatic stance on magical force - not wishing to stake a claim on some quite-possibly false notion of this magical force as material and empirically verifiable - as the first-hand experience of this "force" or "energy" and its various results when directed are what matter (pun not intended).

II. WHAT DOES MAGICAL ENERGY FEEL LIKE?

Celebrants of the Mass often speak of "moving energy" or "feeling the energy" (or the lack thereof). While there is absolutely no mention thereof in the actual rubric of the Gnostic Mass[16], it is not surprising that Magicians - familiar with other forms of ceremonial magick in theory & practice - will see various opportunities for "energy work" in the ritual.

The experience of "energy" itself is going to be unique to each individual, just as any one person's experience of anything will be different from another's. Nonetheless, there are some common threads that seem to at least be somewhat universal.

What appears to be the most universal first-hand sense of energy is a sense of heat. This is unsurprising as there are parallels in other traditions; the most obvious is the Hindu notion of *tapas*

---

16 It may be that something amounting to this might be intended by the note in the rubric, "Certain secret formulæ of this Mass are taught to the PRIEST in his Ordination"; unfortunately it seems we will never know what was meant by that phrase. Sabazius notes, "Some commentators have alleged that these Certain Secret Formulae are none other than the secrets of the Ninth Degree O.T.O. Obviously, this cannot be the case if the Priest being ordained is not an initiate of the Ninth Degree of O.T.O. However, certain secret formulae of this Mass are set forth in certain of the essays herein," by which he presumably means the Tetragrammaton (YHVH) and Pentagrammaton (YHShVH) as they are the two formulae to which he refers often.

which refers to spiritual austerities (including mantra, concentration, etc.). The term *tapas* literally means "heat" and it is by the various spiritual practices that a yogi generates the "spiritual heat" of aspiration. This is paralleled in a Holy Book of Thelema where a similar idea is spoken to using alchemical imagery: "...in the alembic of this spiritual alchemy, if only the zelator blow sufficiently upon his furnace all the systems of earth are consumed in the One Knowledge."[17]

Aside from the symbolic notion of "spiritual heat," energy is felt as a literal heat in the body, and can even lead to a certain type of sweat. This is spoken of in the context of practicing *pranayama* (which we earlier saw is essentially the practice of controlling "magical energy" through manipulation of the breath), where Crowley writes, "If Pranayama be properly performed, the body will first of all become covered with sweat. This sweat is different in character from that customarily induced by exertion. If the Practitioner rub this sweat thoroughly into his body, he will greatly strengthen it."[18]

This sweat is mentioned in LIBER AL and echoed in the Gnostic Mass itself when the Priest says "...the dew of her light bathing his whole body in a sweet-smelling perfume of sweat."[19] Notably, at this point, the entire Congregation along with the Deacon and Children are all in a pose of adoration on their knees with their hands raised above their hands like little flames of illumination, the *tapas* or "spiritual heat" by which the Priest's aspiration is led to the Veil to rend it. In practice, one might feel one's body filled with heat, one's face might become flushed, one's arms and legs might seem to be particularly warm, and it seems to be particularly pronounced if one is focusing attention upon a particular point of the body (e.g. the area of the breast or heart might become especially warm if focusing thereon).

Energy is also experienced in other ways. The most

---

17 *Liber Porta Lucis.*
18 *Liber RV vel Spiritus.*
19 *Liber AL,* I:27.

common other than a sense of heat - although often connected thereto - is the feeling of "chills" or one's hair "standing on end." Another is a feeling of lightheaded-ness, similar to when one's body is overheated from exertion, although this sense in particular may indicate that one's "vessel" is not strong enough to contain the "energy." As it is said in LIBER AL, II:70, "Wisdom says: be strong! Then canst thou bear more joy."

Heat, chills, and light-headedness are all particularly sensory or visceral experiences connected with the experience of energy. There are also more "perceptual" changes such as the contraction of focus or expansion of awareness, often occurring in Priest or Priestess respectively. There are, no doubt, other ways in which energy might be felt – it may be felt as a sharp shock, an electric impulse, a diffuse warmth, or really anything else: there is no reason to exclude *a priori* any particular manifestations of magical energy. The only way one can be certain how they are going to experience it is to simply be mindful while engaging in ritual in order to become aware of changes in sensation and perception that might accompany this "moving of energy."

III. HOW DO WE USE MAGICAL ENERGY?

We have treated the theoretical and experiential sides of "magical energy" or "magical power," yet the practical question remains: how might the Magician generate and employ this energy to their ritualistic ends

Pranayama

As to the generation of magical energy, one method has been mentioned repeatedly thus far: *pranayama*. This includes the formal practice of *pranayama* wherein one sits in a determined posture, or *asana,* and breaths for very specific counts of exhalation, inhalation, and retention for a specific amount of time. Nonetheless, we might include any method that intentionally alters the breathing pattern under the heading of *pranayama*.

The use of breath in the Mass is something that is not written into the rubric itself, but many traditions have been passed down through word of mouth. It is an important means of accessing "magical energy" in the celebration of the Mass, and further details as to how the various Officers of the Mass might employ breath will be treated in the next section of this essay.

Visualization

Visualization is another primary vehicle of generating magical energy. The visualization of various things – including Light, energy, symbols, and so on – can be used to generate magical energy. For example, during the lifting of the Lance, the Priest might visualize the shaft of the Lance as being imbued with electric energy which is emitted in a great Light from the tip of the Lance; or: during the consecration of the Host, the Priest might visualize energy descending from the Lance into the Host to make it the Body of God. Regardless of the content of visualization, the act of visualizing is another source of magical energy for the celebrants of the Mass.

Invocation

The generation of magical energy is also done in anything that is an invocation of any type. Along with the more explicit invocations such as the "Thou who art I..." of the Anthem, there are more subtle invocations such as the circumambulations of the Temple by various Officers, the use of Words of Powers (AUMGN and IAO are the most frequent in the Mass), and certain gestures (the Cross, or "the Sign of Light", is the most frequently used invocatory gesture as well as the stroking of the Lance, various touches and kisses, etc.)

Sexuality

A special "type" or "class" of invocation would be those of a sexual nature. We have already seen the intimate link between the notion of magical energy and sexual force, and the Gnostic Mass definitely utilizes at least the symbolic enactment of sexuality to effect its ends. Therefore, the parts of the Mass that are particularly "sexual" in nature can be seen as specifically focused on the generation or discharge of magical power through the vehicle of sexual expression. The stroking of the Lance eleven times, the raising of the Lance, the piercing of the Veil by the Lance, the nakedness of the Priestess and the Priest's the adoration thereof during the Collects, and the identification of the particle of the Host with the Priest's sperm are all fairly explicit examples of the wedding of sexual force to the invocation of magical energy in the Mass. The simultaneous orgasm of "HRILIU" from both Priest and Priestess depressing the Lance into the Cup is an explicit example of the discharge of magical energy through sexual symbolism.

Regardless of details, the sexual nature of the Mass has the potential to generate sexual energy - to generate desire, passion, magnetism, and similarly sexually-charged sensations - that can be consciously controlled and directed as magical force proper.

Concentration

Ultimately, all of these various techniques for the generation of magical energy must come under the general technique of concentration, or focused attention. It is the concentration of the Magician that gives magical power its purpose, control, and direction. It is the difference between simply lighting a fire and lighting a fire to be used for cooking food, between discharging electricity and the directed use of electricity to power something.

It is stated unambiguously in LIBER LIBRAE: "To obtain Magical Power, learn to control thought; admit only those ideas that are in harmony with the end desired, and not every stray and contradictory Idea that presents itself." The prerequisite to the channeling of magical energy or power in the Mass (or in any ritual) is therefore the ability to concentrate the mind, to control thought, to limit focus to the task at hand without distraction. There is an unknown and possibly infinite degree to which one might hone one's concentration skills, so it is unreasonable to expect someone to be an "expert" before attempting to "move energy" in the Mass or other rituals. Nonetheless, a general foundation of skill in concentration is the necessary basis for the successful generation and direction of magical energy. This is the reason for Crowley's warning:

"The Magician may easily be overwhelmed and obsessed by the force which he has let loose; it will then probably manifest itself in its lowest and most objectionable form. The most intense spirituality of purpose is absolutely essential to safety (This is a matter of concentration, with no ethical implication. The danger is that one may get something which one does not want. This is 'bad' by definition. Nothing is in itself good or evil.)" [20]

This concentration one thing - or "intense spirituality of purpose" - becomes especially important when utilizing forces such as sexuality, for which our conditioned habit is to descend into pure animalistic indulgence rather than the transmutation thereof to effect magical ends.

It should be noted, in concluding this section, that there are doubtless plenty of other means to generate magical energy. The list is not intended to be exhaustive, but the most common and obvious cases have been noted above.

Summary

We have seen that magical energy is generated through work with the breath (*pranayama*), visualization, invocation, and sexuality. We have also seen that magical energy is directed through the power of concentration or focus of attention. Anyone who wanted to become more proficient and utilizing magical energy in the Mass, or in any ritual, would do well to engage in exercises that strengthen the core faculties of breath control, visualization, and concentration[21], and a general familiarity with one's own ability to "enflame oneself in prayer" through invocation, sexual or otherwise, is obviously beneficial as well. For the more advanced student, the study of certain Holy Books is recommended to supplement one's understanding, especially LIBER A'ASH VEL CAPRICORNI PNEUMATICI, LIBER STELLAE RUBEAE, and portions of LIBER AL.

---

20 *Magick in Theory & Practice,* chapter 12.
21 *Liber E* gives practices for pranayama and concentration.

IV. How might the Officers employ Magical Energy in the Mass?

We now have a basic skeleton of understanding of magical energy, both in theory & practice. We have seen that magical energy - also known as "magical force" and "magical power" - was known under various names such as the life-force, *prana, Aud, kundalini,* and Phallus; that it resides in both men and women; and that ultimately we may not (or may never) know of its true nature, but we may work with it in a pragmatic way where certain results occur from certain actions. We have seen that magical energy is typically felt as heat, chills, light-headed-ness, and the expansion / contraction of awareness. Practically, we have seen that magical energy can be generated through breath, visualization, invocation, and sexuality and it is channeled through concentration. All of these ideas form the building blocks from which we may construct an understanding of how we might go about generating and directing magical energy in the Mass.

This discussion will not be exhaustive as there are as many ways to work with energy in the Mass as there are individuals (or, perhaps, as many as there are different permutations of different "Mass teams"). These are merely suggestive, to give directions of inquiry and experiment for each individual to experiment. If there is one universal piece of advice I might offer, it is that - regardless of whatever it is one is doing - there should be a *reason* for doing it. There should be an *intention* guiding the actions, and the only way to truly "do it wrong" is to generate and direct energy without any particular aim or rationale. It is the fact that energy is *controlled* and *directed* that makes it the power of a Magician, one who causes Change in conformity with Will, rather than simply any person off the street.

Children

The Children of the Mass have no speaking roles within the ritual, which leads to many feeling like participating in the role of Child is not much more than acting as "Temple furniture." First of all, the lack of speaking roles gives the Children the opportunity to focus exclusively - at least at first - on proper posture (remaining in the Attitude of Resurrection for long periods is definitely it's own *asana* practice!), moving in a mirrored fashion with one another, and learning to adapt to the unexpected which inevitably occurs. These things are all worthwhile practices in themselves and the skills they strengthen will undoubtedly aid the individual in their eventual celebration as Deacon and/or as Priest/Priestess.

On top of this, the role of Child is a perfect place to start to begin to experiment and work with magical energy. We can, in fact, see the role of Children as being that of the Priest and Priestess but "on a lower octave," just like the Prince and Princess of Tetragrammaton may grow to become the King and Queen. The "Positive Child" and "Negative Child" can then work with energy between themselves as do the Priest and Priestess with each other. It might be noted that the "energy flow" of the Priest and Priestess is almost entirely "vertical" if we imagine looking down on the Gnostic Mass temple with the High Altar at the top (corresponding to the Supernals of the Tree of Life). The Children's "energy flow" between each other is then almost entirely "horizontal," balancing out that of the Priest and Priestess.

Whatever the Children decide to do in terms of working with magical energy, they should decide together before the Mass begins. Regardless of what specific work is being done, it should ideally be paralleled or mirrored by the other Child for the sake of symbolic and magical equilibrium within the Temple. What follows are several examples of what the Children *might* do if they were to attempt to work with magical energy. This is obviously not official in any way: the examples are meant to be purely suggestive, to help Children to figure out something they might experiment with in order that they might find what works best for them.

Firstly, the Children may focus on their breath. The breath should be made deeper and longer, although I firmly caution against straining and/or jerkiness with breathing. This intentional breathing alone is a worthwhile practice, and might be profitably experimented with for several Masses without any other additions.

One might add the visualization of imagining that, when inhaling, one is drawing in the breath of the other Child and, when exhaling, one is "feeding" the other Child with one's own breath. This "cycle" of energy is, in general, a typical pattern of energy work as it represents a dynamic equilibrium, and the foundation of all Magick is equilibrium. Further, the "cycling" can act as a sort of motor or feedback loop, where the continuous cycling of energy has the effect of feeling that the energy is getting stronger, warmer, more intense, and similar sensations. This general principle can be extended to virtually any energy work between two individuals, including but not limited to the Priest and Priestess.

One might add other visualizations on top of the breathing and cycling. For example, I have heard of the Negative Child visualizing that they inhale the breath from the Positive Child (cycling), but the exhale is visualized as a waterfall that rushes as a river over to the Positive Child. The Positive Child then visualizes inhaling this "river," bringing up the energy through the body, and exhaling it like a volcano expelling fire into the atmosphere. The fire and air travels over to the Negative Child who inhales it, *et cetera.* Another example I have heard has been the Negative Child visualizing a typical Water triangle (apex downward) between the two Children, while the Positive Child visualizes a typical Fire triangle (apex upward); together, their visualizations form the Hexagram of union in the middle. My personal preference is to simply focus upon breath and the simple visualization of cycling breath, but it may be advantageous to certain individuals to have more complex visualizations, even if only to practice the faculty of visualization while Child-ing.

Communion is a time that is ripe for energy work, aside from the rest of the Mass where the Children are virtually always facing each other and can be practicing cycling breath or other forms of energy work. The Children can, of course, continue their energy cycling between one another. I personally prefer to focus my attention on the Communicants as they come up, since - at this point in the ritual - they are the central focus. There are nearly infinite options of what to do at this point, but here are some examples.

One might cycle breath with the other Child in between Communicants coming up to the High Altar, and then focus one's energy upon the Communicant, directing energy to their hearts, their Solar center.

One might also channel the energy into the Cake of Light and goblet of Wine that the Communicant receives, infusing it with even more magical energy. Since the offerings are of Life (Cake of Light) and Joy (Wine), the Positive Child can mentally say "I am Life and the giver of Life" while focusing on the Cake of Light the Communicant is retrieving and consuming. The Negative Child might mentally say "Remember all ye that existence is pure joy" while focusing on the Wine the Communicant is retrieving and consuming.

One might even completely stop "energy work" during Communication and simply give one's focused attention to the Communicant as they partake of the Eucharist. All of these, again, are simply suggestions to get one's own thoughts going as to how one might use magical energy in the Mass as a Child.

Deacon

The Deacon also has many opportunities to work with magical energy during the Gnostic Mass. It has been noted, though, that the work of the Deacon is actually unlike the Children or the Priest and Priestess in a specific way, which is that the Deacon must keep what Tau Polyphilus called "surface presence."[22] The Deacon cannot simply get lost in the energy like Children or like the Priest and Priestess tend to do, because he is responsible for the People and the Temple in general. He is, in this way, the "magician" of the Mass - or even the "ego" of the Mass - which has to make sure that the candles are all lit, there are enough wines for Communion, that disruptive people are dealt with accordingly, that someone having a coughing fit gets some water, or deal with the infinite other things

---

22 See "Advice for Deacons" by Tau Polyphilus.

that can (and have and will) go awry during a Mass.

Nonetheless, there are still many times to work with magical energy as Deacon. The following list is, once again, simply suggestive instead of comprehensive. The Deacon begins with the "magical weapon" of THE BOOK OF THE LAW. The Deacon can imagine holding the Word of God, or Logos, in their hands as they approach the High Altar with reverence. After bowing, the Deacon can take a deep breath and infuse the Book with energy through their three kisses. Upon placing the Book on the super-altar, the Deacon may turn and project out this Logos through their pronouncement to the Congregation. During the recitation of the Creed, the Deacon can visualize the entire Temple forming like a new Universe, and the words of the Creed filling the Universe with its various laws and energy and motion. When handed the Priest's Lance, the Deacon can visualize that they are holding a super-charged Promethean rod of divine Phallic energy. During the Saints Collect, the Deacon can visualize the crosses being traced on the Cup which holds the blood of the saints, or upon the back of the Priest as a successor and heir of the Saints. As a side note, one should always check with others if one is going to do visualizations such as this – the Deacon might simply ask if it would be alright to draw the crosses on the Priest's back during the Saints or whether they have any preference themselves. There are, of course, many other opportunities for the Deacon to utilize magical energy during the Mass, but I will leave them up to the reader's own ingenium and experience to find those which most authentically express their own magical ideals.

Priest & Priestess

The Priest and Priestess are naturally the Officers of the Gnostic Mass that most obviously work with magical energy. Every step the Priest or Priestess takes, every word they speak, every gesture they make are all infused with the potentiality of great magical power. There are innumerable ways the Priest and Priestess can make use of magical energy in the Mass – far too numerous to even begin to mention the many possibilities. I will note that "breath work" between the Priest and Priestess is likely the best foundation for "moving" the energy of the Mass. There are several points where this is particularly natural and efficacious:

1) When the Priestess kneels to stroke the Lance eleven times, this gives an opportunity for the Priest and Priestess to breathe in harmony with one another and with the stroking of the Lance.

2) During the Collects, when the Priest is adoring the Priestess on his knees, there is ample opportunity for working with breath and energy. This is an especially good time to "turn up" the energy, as there are no words or actions for either Priest or Priestess to worry about during this period.

3) During the *commixto* of Particle and Wine, there can be a moment of conjoined breath-work between the Priest and Priestess before the "HRILIU."

It might be added that the Priest "breathing with" the Priestess can mean many things. The two simplest meanings of this are (a) inhaling & exhaling at the same time as one another, or (b) inhaling while the other exhales and vice versa. My personal preference is the latter, as it reflects a cyclic motion of breath and energy similar to that recommended previously for the Children. What works best must, as always, be a result of one's own personal experimentation and experience as well as the collaboration with what one's Priest/Priestess is comfortable with.

V. CONCLUSION

In concluding this article, I wish to once again firmly impress upon the mind of the reader that this essay is not meant to include all aspects of "magical energy," either in theory or in practice. An entire book could (and should!) be written on such things.

This essay's intention is simply to bring the awareness of individuals to the deeper aspects of our work in the central rite of our Holy Order.

Nothing I have said is absolute, nor is it meant to be. The various suggestions for energy work are just that: suggestions. I believe in "The Method of Science," so I heartily encourage you to experiment with various approaches and see what works for yourself.

As a final reminder, I believe we must always remember that all these discussions, all these ideas, all these experiments, and exercises are all (ideally) in order to deepen our experience of the Gnostic Mass, to further appreciate its manifold Mysteries, to bring the Flame of Knowledge more brilliantly to humankind, and to more joyously and beautifully engage in our True Wills.

There is an amazing repository of potential in this beautiful ritual that is simply lying fallow, waiting for the injection of sincere aspirants' earnest intention and zeal. The many veils that blind our perception of the intensity of this ritual's Light are also the portals we may pass through to True Wisdom and Perfect Happiness.

Afterword

Do what thou wilt shall be the whole of the Law!

"Magical Energy in the Gnostic Mass" picks up so many lines, it is not possible to follow them all, not by a single author in a single work. Thus, this essay is a crisis of sorts. IAO131 has pointed in the direction of critical reflection on Thelema by showing us different avenues of investigation. The crisis is that we are now at a place where we can threaten Thelemic "orthodoxies," secure in our gnosis and unafraid of the facts. We can rebel, as we should if we are to be true to the spirit of Thelema. If we refuse to attack (and defend, via the use of facts and experience) the common human trend toward orthodoxy, we will be overtaken by the crisis. Critical theoretical work is necessary to confront the crisis and transmute it into an opportunity.

To illustrate the crisis, take the dual claims of IAO131 that "In the Hindu understanding, the sexual force is but one form [of magickal energy]... [W]e recognize the sexual Force as the potent manifestation of magical force in general". These claims are rather straightforward and generally accepted within the Thelemic community. A whole host of concerns come to mind here. For instance, the idea that a unitary concept of magical force shows up in the various religious traditions of the world under a number of guises is debatable. Paying attention to the similarities of Kundalini, prana, chi, ki, and ruach without asking how the concepts diverge can only give the illusion of agreement. IAO131 seems to suggest that the various concepts of magical force are fungible even if they are different (and so he does, at least tacitly, recognize the problem of divergence for the account of magical energy he is offering us). Along that line of thinking he cites Crowley's "Energized Enthusiasm": "the sexual excitement must be suppressed and transformed into its religious equivalent." Similarly, IAO131 notes that control of the breath leads to control of prana; a physical element is transfigured into a spiritual power.

The question must be raised at this point as to what a power or an energy or a force is.

Sexual energy is the rush of neurotransmitters and other physiological events. It is not actually an energy strictly speaking but a subjective experience of objective processes. Similarly, the control of the breath may lead to psychological and physiological consequences such as sweating or a feeling of expansion or a sense of time contracting. But none of those consequences are recognizable as a form of energy. The consequences are, instead, symptoms rather than evidence of a force which can do work.

The crisis then (one of many created by IAO131's magnificent work) is this: at least on the face of it, the language of magical energy misleads us into a false sense of understanding. Magical energy is not a single, well-defined concept nor does it have any outstanding features that would allow us to distinguish magical energy as anything more than physiology and psychology. The occult orthodoxy that takes literally and historically reports of magical feats and conjuring demons, the effects of the use of magical energy, appears grounded in a concept that is not developed enough to support the orthodox doctrine. But this is not the last word on the matter nor the only moment of crisis in IAO131's work. Can we carry on our magical work and be fulfilled by it if we abandon the orthodox understanding of magical power?

The fact is that magicians have some sort of experience that leads them to talk about magical energy. Comparative religion and psychology are areas that can ground our inquiries into the matter. Practice can also ground our inquiries if we are attentive and careful to characterize our magical work. In my own opinion, bhakti yoga, the path of devotion, gives the magician a powerful means of delving into our work and experiencing a mystical and magical world, even if that world remains simply what it is we started with, the mundane. Care must be taken, as was said earlier, to avoid the mistake of taking one's own path for the only path. Care must also be given to appreciating our experiences for what they are: a quiet, simple, and often deep and inarticulable encounter. (This is the way it is with true secrets.) In this way, we will find joy in our aimless winging.

Fraternally,

Frater Yeheshuah

Love is the law, love under will.

www.ingramcontent.com/pod-product-compliance
Lightning Source LLC
Chambersburg PA
CBHW031531040426

42445CB00009B/490